RAND | NATIONAL DEFENSE RESEARCH INSTITUTE

SEXUAL ASSAULT AND SEXUAL HARASSMENT IN THE U.S. MILITARY

Top-Line Estimates for Active-Duty Service Members from the 2014 RAND Military Workplace Study

National Defense Research Institute

Prepared for the DoD Sexual Assault Prevention and Response Office

For more information on this publication, visit www.rand.org/t/RR870

Library of Congress Cataloging-in-Publication Data is available for this publication.
ISBN: 978-0-8330-8859-8

Support RAND
Make a tax-deductible charitable contribution at
www.rand.org/giving/contribute

www.rand.org

The 2014 RAND Military Workplace Study Team

Principal Investigators
Andrew R. Morral, Ph.D.
Kristie L. Gore, Ph.D.

Instrument Design
Lisa Jaycox, Ph.D., team lead
Terry Schell, Ph.D.
Coreen Farris, Ph.D.
Dean Kilpatrick, Ph.D.*
Amy Street, Ph.D.*
Terri Tanielian, M.A.*

Study Design and Analysis
Terry Schell, Ph.D., team lead
Bonnie Ghosh-Dastidar, Ph.D.
Marc Elliott, Ph.D.
Craig Martin, M.A.
Mark Totten, M.S.
Q Burkhart, M.S.
Robin Beckman, M.P.H.

Project Management
Kayla M. Williams, M.A.
Caroline Epley, M.P.A.
Amy Grace Peele, M.P.P.

Survey Coordination
Jennifer Hawes-Dawson

Westat Survey Group
Shelley Perry, Ph.D., team lead
Wayne Hintze, M.S.
John Rauch
Bryan Davis
Lena Watkins
Richard Sigman, M.S.
Michael Hornbostel, M.S.

Project Communications
Steve Kistler
Jeffrey Hiday
Barbara Bicksler, M.P.P.

Scientific Advisory Board

Major General John Altenburg, Esq. (USA, ret.)
Captain Thomas A. Grieger, M.D. (USN, ret.)
Dean Kilpatrick, Ph.D.
Laura Miller, Ph.D.
Amy Street, Ph.D.
Roger Tourangeau, Ph.D.

David Cantor, Ph.D.
Colonel Dawn Hankins, USAF
Roderick Little, Ph.D.
Sharon Smith, Ph.D.
Terri Tanielian, M.A.
Veronica Venture, J.D.

* Three members of the Scientific Advisory Board were so extensively involved in the development of the survey instrument that we list them here as full Instrument Design team members.

Contents

Figures and Tables

Summary

In early 2014, the Department of Defense (DoD) Sexual Assault Prevention and Response Office (SAPRO) asked the RAND National Defense Research Institute (NDRI) to conduct an independent assessment of sexual assault, sexual harassment, and gender discrimination in the military—an assessment last conducted in 2012 by the department itself through the Workplace and Gender Relations Survey of Active Duty Personnel (WGRA). This report provides preliminary top-line estimates from the resulting study, the RAND Military Workplace Study (RMWS), which invited close to 560,000 service members to participate in a survey fielded in August and September of 2014.

Compared to the prior DoD studies, the RMWS takes a new approach to counting individuals in the military who experienced sexual assault, sexual harassment, or gender discrimination. Our measurement of sexual assault aligns closely with the definitions and criteria in the Uniform Code of Military Justice (UCMJ) for Article 120 and Article 80 crimes. The survey measures of sexual harassment and gender discrimination, which together we refer to as sex-based military equal opportunity (MEO) violations, use criteria drawn directly from DoD Directive 1350.2. Compared with past surveys that were designed to measure a climate of sexual misconduct associated with illegal behavior, our approach offers greater precision in estimating the number of *crimes* and *MEO violations* that have occurred. Specifically, the RMWS measures

- *Sexual assault*, which captures three mutually exclusive categories: *penetrative*, *non-penetrative*, and *attempted penetrative* crimes
- *Sex-based MEO violations*, which consist of
  - *Sexually hostile work environment*—a workplace characterized by persistent or severe unwelcome sexual advances, or verbal or physical conduct that offends service members
  - *Sexual quid pro quo*—incidents in which someone uses his or her power or influence within the military to attempt to coerce sexual behavior in exchange for a workplace benefit
  - *Gender discrimination*—incidents in which service members are subject to mistreatment on the basis of their gender that affects their employment conditions.

As with all crime-victim surveys, we classify service members as experiencing these crimes or MEO violations based on their memories of the event as expressed in their survey responses. It is likely that a full review of all evidence would reveal that some respondents whom we classify as not having experienced a sexual assault or sex-based MEO violation based on their survey responses actually did have one of these experiences. Similarly, some whom we classify as having experienced a crime or violation may have experienced an event that would not meet the minimum legal criteria. A principal focus of our survey development was to minimize both of these types of errors, but they cannot be completely eliminated in a self-report survey.

Subject to these caveats, we estimate with 95-percent confidence that between 18,000 and 22,500 active-duty service members can be classified as having experienced one or more sexual assaults in the past year committed against them by other service members, civilians, spouses, or others. Our best estimate in this range is that approximately 20,000 active-duty service members were sexually assaulted in the past year, out of 1,317,561 active-duty members. This represents approximately 1.0 percent of active-duty men and 4.9 percent of active-duty women. Moreover, the nature of these sexual assaults appears to be different than estimated using the earlier survey methods: 43 percent of assaults against women and 35 percent of assaults against men were classified as penetrative sexual assaults. These figures are higher than comparable estimates we generated using the WGRA methods for counting penetrative sexual assaults, and this difference is particularly large among men.

Our estimates suggest high rates of sex-based MEO violations against active-duty women, more than a quarter of whom may have experienced a sex-based MEO violation in the past year. Among women in the Navy and Marines, the rate of MEO violations approaches one-third. The majority of these violations involve experiences consistent with a sexually hostile work environment; however, significant numbers of women also indicate experiences consistent with gender discrimination.

Our estimate of the prevalence of sex-based MEO violations against active-duty men is lower than for women, but these are higher than estimates we produced using the WGRA methods for measuring sexual harassment. Moreover, these problems are cited sufficiently often to warrant attention. For example, we estimate that in the Army, almost 1 in 12 men experienced a sex-based MEO violation in the past year; in the Navy, it was nearly 1 in 10. For men, the largest source of problems stem from sexually hostile work environments.

Recognizing that DoD is also interested in trends in sexual assault, sexual harassment, and gender discrimination, RAND fielded a portion of the 2014 surveys using the same questions as previous DoD surveys on this topic. Our findings suggest that unwanted sexual contact and sexual harassment, as these have been measured over the past eight years, have declined for active-duty women since 2012. We estimate that the percentage of active-duty women who experienced unwanted sexual contact as measured by the WGRA methods declined from 6.1 percent in 2012 to 4.3 percent in 2014;

the same percentages for men did not see a statistically significant change (1.2 percent in 2012 compared with 0.9 percent in 2014). Similarly, estimates for the percentage of women who experienced sexual harassment in the past year declined significantly from 23.2 percent in 2012 to 20.2 percent in 2014; for men, the percentage in 2014 (3.5 percent) was not significantly lower than in 2012 (4.1 percent). The trend data suggest that fewer active-duty service women are experiencing unwanted sexual contacts and sexual harassment than was the case two years ago, but significant improvements over 2010 levels have not occurred. Women's experiences with retaliation after filing an official report to a military authority are unchanged in 2014. In both 2012 and 2014, 62 percent who filed such a report indicated that they experienced professional retaliation, social retaliation, adverse administrative actions, or punishments for violations associated with the sexual assault.

This report includes only preliminary top-line findings for active-duty personnel from the RAND Military Workplace Study, reporting on the broadest categories of outcomes (by service, gender, and type of offense). These top-line results are likely to generate many questions about the details of the sexual assaults and MEO violations we have documented here, as well as about differences in estimates produced using the prior form and the new questionnaire. The RAND team will continue to analyze these and other topics in the winter of 2014–2015. Reports summarizing the findings from these analyses will be released in the late spring of 2015.

Introduction

In early 2014, the Department of Defense (DoD) asked the RAND National Defense Research Institute to conduct an independent assessment of sexual assault, sexual harassment, and gender discrimination in the military—an assessment last conducted in 2012 by the department itself through the Workplace and Gender Relations Survey of Active Duty Personnel (WGRA). The 2014 RAND Military Workplace Study (RMWS) is based on a much larger sample of the military community than previous surveys—men and women, active-duty and reserve component, and including the four DoD military services plus the Coast Guard—and is designed to more precisely estimate the total number of service members experiencing sexual assault, sexual harassment, and gender discrimination.

The objectives of the 2014 survey were to

- establish precise and objective estimates of the percentage of service members who experience sexual assault, sexual harassment, and gender discrimination
- describe the characteristics of these incidents, such as where and when they occurred, who harassed or assaulted the member, whether the event was reported, and what services the member sought
- identify barriers to reporting these incidents and barriers to the receipt of support and legal services.

To meet its December 1, 2014, deadline for providing the White House a report documenting DoD progress in its efforts to prevent and respond to sexual assaults and harassment, the Sexual Assault Prevention and Response Office (SAPRO) in the Office of the Secretary of Defense (OSD) requested that RAND report top-line estimates on the DoD active-duty sample shortly after the survey field period closed. These *top-line* numbers refer to the broadest categories of outcomes and include only estimated numbers and percentages of service members who experienced sexual assault, sexual harassment, and gender discrimination in the past year by gender, service, and type of offense. Because we randomly assigned some respondents to complete the new questionnaire designed by RAND and a smaller number to complete a version of the prior 2012 WGRA questionnaire, we are able to provide top-line estimates using both the earlier assessment criteria and methods and the newly designed assessment criteria and methods. This allows comparisons between 2012 and 2014 and also provides new estimates based on the revised questionnaire, which has several methodological advantages described below.

In addition to the preliminary top-line numbers presented here, the RAND research team will conduct additional analyses on the survey data and will include those findings in reports that are planned for release in the late spring of 2015. These reports will examine the experiences of victims with the response systems available to them, their rationale for either reporting or not reporting sexual assaults and harassment to their command or to victim service professionals, and the circumstances of their experiences (such as who harassed or assaulted them, where and when it happened, and whether they experienced retaliation). In addition, we will provide detailed documentation on our methodology and study approach.

A New Approach to Counting Sexual Assault, Sexual Harassment, and Gender Discrimination

DoD has assessed service members' experiences with sexual assault and harassment since at least 1996, when Public Law 104-201 first required a survey of the "gender relations climate" experienced by active-duty forces. Since 2002, four "Workplace and Gender Relations Surveys," as they are known in 10 USC §481, have been conducted with active-duty forces (in 2002, 2006, 2010, and 2012). The DoD conducted reserve-component versions of this survey in 2004, 2008, and 2012.

The results of the 2012 survey suggested that more than 26,000 active-duty service members had experienced "unwanted sexual contact" in the prior year, an estimate that received widespread public attention and concern. In press reports and congressional inquiries, questions were raised about the validity of the estimate, about what "unwanted sexual contact" included, and about whether the survey had been conducted properly. Some of these concerns and criticisms were unfounded. Although there are significant differences in our approach, the earlier WGRA survey did employ many of the same best practices for survey research that we have adopted for the RMWS (Office of Management and Budget, 2006). However, these concerns led some members of Congress to urge DoD to seek a new and independent assessment of the number of service members exposed to sexual assault or sexual harassment across the military.

In selecting RAND to conduct the 2014 assessment, DoD sought a new and independent evaluation of sexual assault, sexual harassment, and gender discrimination across the military. As such, DoD encouraged the RAND research team to redesign the approach used previously in the WGRA surveys if changes would improve the accuracy and validity of the survey results for estimating crimes and violations. In developing the new RMWS questionnaire, RAND researchers were conscious of the challenges of measuring sexual assault, sexual harassment, and gender discrimination. For example, seemingly slight changes in the descriptions of these events can substantially influence survey results. Therefore, the RAND questions assessing sexual assault closely track the definitions and criteria listed in the Uniform Code of Military Justice (UCMJ) for Article 120 crimes. Likewise, our approach to measuring sexual harassment and gender discrimination was designed to closely align with the definitions of those violations as described in DoD directives, which themselves are closely aligned with federal civil rights law.[1]

To better assess the prevalence of sexual assault, sexual harassment, and gender discrimination, we sought to develop simple sets of questions that could be used to correctly classify respondents' experiences according to the complex criteria set out in law. In addition to breaking down complex legal standards into a series of questions amenable to a self-administered survey format, we also sought to introduce technical changes to improve respondent comprehension of the survey questions, and in turn to enhance the validity of their answers.

The development of this new approach to measuring sexual assault and sex-based MEO violations was completed in close consultation with a scientific advisory board that included experts on civilian and military law, the assessment of sexual assault and sexual harassment, victim services, and survey methodology. In addition, RAND researchers consulted with many other experts, advocacy groups, and service members, including many who had experienced sexual assault or sexual harassment, to ensure that each survey question assessed the legal construct it was designed to measure as accurately as possible and to ensure that respondents could reliably understand the meaning of each question.

Thus, the RMWS survey is designed to provide a valid and precise estimate of the number of service men and women who have experienced sexual assault, sexual harassment, or gender discrimination in the past year. It more closely links survey definitions of sexual offenses to the law than the WGRA did. Other improvements in our survey approach include

- **Simplifying question syntax to improve respondent understanding.** Earlier WGRA surveys used complex questions for the sexual harassment and unwanted sexual contact measures, questions that placed heavy demands on respondents' reading skills and comprehension. RAND's approach presented a series of questions asking about behaviorally specific experiences.
- **Clarifying question terminology.** The prior WGRA approach to measuring sexual assault relied on respondents' understanding of the complex concept of *consent*, and did so without defining the term. The RAND questionnaire avoids use of the term consent for most definitions of sexual assault. Instead, we substituted the behaviorally specific forms of coercion described in Article 120 of the UCMJ that operationalize the concept of consent. Similarly, we limited use of the term *sexual* in defining the events that might qualify as sexual assault because sexual assaults that would qualify as crimes under Article 120 need not be associated with sexual gratification if they are designed to humiliate or debase the person who is assaulted. Instead, the new RMWS survey inquires about sexual assaults using simple behavioral and anatomical descriptions that make no reference to whether or not the behaviors were "sexual." Use of such behaviorally

and anatomically specific language not only better matches the similarly specific language of Article 120, it has also been the standard approach for accurately assessing sexual assault in survey research conducted with civilian populations for decades (National Research Council, 2014). We believe these changes (and many others like them) clarify the meaning and intent of our survey questions and have improved the reliability and validity of the respondents' answers. Pretesting of the survey indicated that respondents found the items to be clear and easy to understand.

- **Reducing overcounting of offenses due to telescoping.** People often report crimes as occurring more recently than they really did—a tendency that is referred to as *response telescoping*. To guard against this phenomenon, RAND implemented several strategies in the RMWS survey that are designed to better orient respondents to the specific timeframe under consideration in each section of the survey.

All of the improvements in the RMWS survey are designed to provide reliable estimates of the numbers of service members who experienced sexual assault crimes and sex-based MEO violations, and to minimize errors due to overreporting (such as due to response telescoping), and underreporting (such as due to confusion over what counts as a crime). Nevertheless, as with all crime-victim surveys, we classify service members as experiencing these violations based on their memories of the event as expressed in their survey responses. Thus, despite our efforts to reduce many sources of error in our estimates, such errors cannot be completely eliminated in a self-report survey.

Fielding the RAND Military Workplace Study Survey

DoD, in consultation with the White House National Security Staff, stipulated that the sample size for the RMWS was to include a census of all active-duty women and 25 percent of active-duty men in the Army, Navy, Air Force, and Marine Corps. In addition, we were asked to include a smaller sample of National Guard and reserve members sufficient to support comparisons of sexual assault and harassment between the active-duty and reserve forces. Subsequently, the U.S. Coast Guard also asked that RAND include a sample of their active-duty and reserve members.[2] In total, therefore, RAND invited close to 560,000 service members to participate in the study, making it the largest study of sexual assault and harassment ever conducted in the military.

The large sample for this study is particularly valuable for understanding the experiences of relatively small subgroups in the population. For instance, in the smaller 2012 WGRA, 117 men indicated that they experienced what the WGRA defines as "unwanted sexual contact." This low number limits generalizations that can be made about the experiences of men in the military.

The large sample associated with the RMWS also gave RAND the opportunity to test how changing the questionnaire itself might have affected survey results. Specifically, we were able to use a segment of our overall sample to compare rates of exposure to sexual assault and sexual harassment as measured using the 2014 RMWS questionnaire and the 2012 WGRA questionnaire. We achieved this by randomly assigning this portion of the sample to receive questions from the prior WGRA form, while the balance received a version of the new RMWS form.[3]

A total of 477,513 members of the DoD active-duty forces were randomly selected from a population of 1,317,561 active-duty DoD service members who were not reserve component members and who met the study inclusion criteria requiring that they be age 18 or over, below the rank of a general or flag officer, and in service for at least six months.[4] This follows the procedures used in prior WGRA surveys. As noted, sampled service members were randomly assigned to receive either questions from the prior WGRA survey or from one of the new RMWS questionnaires.[5]

The smartphone-compatible, web-based RMWS survey was fielded from August 7, 2014, to September 24, 2014. Before being fielded, the survey instrument underwent significant scientific and ethical review and regulatory approvals by RAND and by several DoD authorities.[6] Service members in the sample were recruited through a series of emails and postal letters sent to them throughout the study period, as well as through outreach activities conducted by RAND, OSD, and service leadership.

The study design contains a range of changes in the survey methods relative to the prior WGRA designed to address critiques of that study. Although many of our innovations build on those developed for the WGRA, the new survey collects more detailed information related to whether the event is consistent with criminal offenses under the UCMJ or violations of MEO. It also includes simpler questions, an experiment to compare the prior WGRA survey and the new RMWS, a larger sample, and an increase in the outreach and recruitment messages. We took three specific steps to increase response rates:

- **A shorter survey.** The RMWS survey that most respondents received is shorter than the prior WGRA and could be completed by most respondents in just eight minutes.
- **Maximizing responses to the key questions.** We placed the sexual assault and sexual harassment modules at the beginning of the survey to maximize the number of respondents answering these questions, since historically there has been considerable survey break-off before reaching these core questions.
- **Reaching junior enlisted members and others with limited access to computers.** We made the survey smartphone compatible and developed a communications plan that promoted the survey through many channels, including social media, public service announcements, and print news stories.

A total of 145,300 active-duty members of DoD services completed the RMWS survey, for a response rate of 30.4 percent.[7]

Top-Line Results from the RAND Military Workplace Study

The Percentage of Active-Duty Men and Women Experiencing Sexual Assault and Harassment

Here we describe the top-line findings on the estimated percentage of active-duty men and women who experienced sexual assaults and sex-based MEO violations (including gender discrimination and sexual harassment) in the past year.[8] Because we measure these offenses differently than they have been measured in the past, the estimates generated using the new RMWS assessment methodology cannot be directly compared with past WGRA results. The results in this section represent our preliminary estimates for the percentage of service members who experienced events in the past year that would qualify as sex crimes under UCMJ Article 120 or Article 80, or sex-based MEO violations.

Sexual Assault

The RMWS survey contains a detailed assessment of sexual assault designed to correspond to the legal criteria specified in UCMJ Article 120. To be classified as having experienced a sexual assault, respondents must first have indicated that they experienced one of six anatomically specific, unwanted behavioral events. If they indicated that one of these events occurred in the past year, they were then asked a series of additional questions designed to assess (a) if the event was intended for either a sexual purpose, to abuse, or to humiliate, and (b) if the offender used one of the coercion methods specified in the UCMJ as defining a criminal sex act.

Using results from the new RMWS survey, we estimate that 1.5 percent of the population experienced at least one sexual assault in the past year (Table 1). We estimate with 95 percent confidence that the total number of service members in our sample frame who experienced a sexual assault in the past year is between 18,000 and 22,500.[9] Our best estimate in this range is that approximately 20,000 active-duty service members were sexually assaulted in the past year, out of 1,317,561 active-duty members. The estimated rate of sexual assault varied dramatically by gender: fewer than 1 in 100 men but approximately 1 in 20 women. There were smaller, yet significant, differences by branch of service, with members of the Air Force (both men and

Table 1
Estimated Percentage of Active-Duty Service Members Who Experienced Any Type of Sexual Assault in the Past Year, by Gender and Service Branch

Service	Total (95% CI)	Male (95% CI)	Female (95% CI)
Total	1.54% (1.38–1.70)	0.95% (0.78–1.15)	4.87% (4.61–5.14)
Army	1.46% (1.25–1.70)	0.95% (0.72–1.23)	4.69% (4.30–5.09)
Navy	2.36%* (1.92–2.86)	1.48% (1.00–2.12)	6.48%* (5.79–7.22)
Air Force	0.78%* (0.70–0.87)	0.29%* (0.21–0.39)	2.90%* (2.67–3.15)
Marines	1.63% (1.15–2.24)	1.13% (0.65–1.84)	7.86%* (6.65–9.21)

* Percentage is significantly different from the average of the other services within a column; p<.05, Bonferroni corrected.

women) estimated to be at lower risk than members of the other branches. In contrast, a significantly higher proportion of women in the Marines and Navy are estimated to have experienced sexual assault in the past year than women in other services.

To gain a better understanding of the nature of these events, we broke down the overall results into the type of sexual assault that the respondent was classified as experiencing (Table 2). The instrument is structured so that if a respondent is classified as having experienced a penetrative sexual assault, they skip the subsequent questions about lesser offenses. Similarly, if they qualify as having experienced a non-penetrative sexual assault, they skip the final questions assessing if they experienced an attempted

Table 2
Estimated Percentage of Active-Duty Service Members Who Experienced a Sexual Assault in the Past Year, by Gender and Type

Sexual Assault	Total (95% CI)	Male (95% CI)	Female (95% CI)
Any sexual assault	1.54% (1.38–1.70)	0.95% (0.78–1.15)	4.87% (4.61–5.14)
Penetrative sexual assault	0.59% (0.49–0.71)	0.33% (0.22–0.48)	2.10% (1.92–2.28)
Non-penetrative sexual assault	0.92% (0.81–1.04)	0.62% (0.50–0.77)	2.60% (2.41–2.81)
Attempted penetrative	0.03% (0.02–0.04)	0.00% (0.00–0.01)	0.19% (0.13–0.26)

penetrative sexual assault. Thus, the instrument defines three mutually exclusive categories of sexual assault: *penetrative*, *non-penetrative*, and *attempted penetrative*.[10]

Penetrative sexual assaults are events that people often refer to as rape. We describe the measure as *penetrative sexual assault* in order to include both penetrative assaults that would be charged as rape and penetrative assaults that would be charged as sexual assault. *Non-penetrative assaults* include incidents in which private areas on the service member's body are touched without penetration, or where the service member is made to have contact with the private areas of another person's body.[11] The *attempted penetrative sexual assault* category applies only to those people who could not be classified with crimes that could be charged directly via Article 120 (*penetrative* or *non-penetrative sexual assaults*). That is, they indicated having experienced an event in which someone attempted to sexually assault them (charged via Article 80), but the person never made physical contact with a private area of their body (which would have allowed categorization under the *non-penetrative sexual assault* category). This approach to classifying sexual assaults results in nearly all sexual assaults being categorized as either *penetrative* or *non-penetrative*, with very few classified as *attempted* assaults.

The distribution across type of assault varies by gender; almost half of all women classified as having experienced a sexual assault indicated the most serious type of crime, *penetrative sexual assault*, while about one-third of the assaulted men indicated the *penetrative* type. Combined with the higher prevalence of sexual assault against women, this means that women are estimated to be at six times the risk of past-year *penetrative* sexual assault relative to men.

The assaults can also be broken down by service and gender within each assault type, as shown in Tables 3 and 4. The overall pattern shown here is similar to what was

Table 3
Estimated Percentage of Active-Duty Service Members Who Experienced Penetrative Sexual Assault in the Past Year, by Gender and Service Branch

Service	Total (95% CI)	Male (95% CI)	Female (95% CI)
Total	0.59% (0.49–0.71)	0.33% (0.22–0.48)	2.10% (1.92–2.28)
Army	0.54% (0.41–0.69)	0.29% (0.17–0.48)	2.05% (1.78–2.34)
Navy	0.81% (0.54–1.15)	0.43% (0.16–0.92)	2.55% (2.13–3.04)
Air Force	0.29%* (0.24–0.34)	0.07%* (0.04–0.12)	1.21%* (1.07–1.38)
Marines	0.90% (0.51–1.48)	0.63% (0.25–1.33)	4.28%* (3.35–5.38)

* Percentage is significantly different from the average of the other services within a column; $p<.05$, Bonferroni corrected.

Table 4
Estimated Percentage of Active-Duty Service Members Who Experienced Non-Penetrative Sexual Assault in the Past Year, by Gender and Service Branch

Service	Total (95% CI)	Male (95% CI)	Female (95% CI)
Total	0.92% (0.81–1.04)	0.62% (0.50–0.77)	2.60% (2.41–2.81)
Army	0.91% (0.74–1.10)	0.65% (0.47–0.88)	2.51% (2.24–2.81)
Navy	1.49%* (1.16–1.89)	1.05%* (0.67–1.55)	3.59% (3.06–4.17)
Air Force	0.48%* (0.41–0.57)	0.22%* (0.15–0.32)	1.62%* (1.45–1.81)
Marines	0.71% (0.47–1.04)	0.50% (0.26–0.87)	3.40% (2.63–4.31)

* Percentage is significantly different from the average of the other services within a column; p<.05, Bonferroni corrected.

seen in the overall measure of sexual assault in Table 2. Men and women in the Air Force are at somewhat lower risk relative to the other services across both measures. There is also evidence of significantly higher estimated percentage of female Marines who experienced a *penetrative sexual assault* and male sailors who experienced a *non-penetrative* assault, relative to members of the same genders in other services.

Sex-Based MEO Violations

As with sexual assault, our measures of sexual harassment and gender discrimination assess a number of specific types of violations. The *sexually hostile work environment* measure is designed to capture a workplace that includes sexual language, gestures, images, or behaviors that offend and anger service members or interfere with their ability to do their jobs. These events are counted only if the offensive behavior is either persistent (e.g., the respondent indicated the behavior continued even after the coworker knows that it is upsetting to others) or described by the respondent as severe (e.g., the behavior is so severe that most service members would find it patently offensive). Table 5 shows that this type of sexual harassment is commonly faced by active-duty service women; we estimate that one-fifth of women experienced upsetting or offensive sexual behavior in the past year that, under federal law or DoD directives, can be classified as an unfair condition of their employment in the military. The pattern of findings also suggests that active-duty members of the Air Force report significantly different experiences than the other branches of service. In particular, the estimated percentage of Air Force members who experienced a *sexually hostile work environment* in the past year was markedly lower than that of other services. Even in this branch,

Table 5
Estimated Percentage of Active-Duty Service Members Who Experienced a Sexually Hostile Work Environment in the Past Year, by Gender and Service Branch

Service	Total (95% CI)	Male (95% CI)	Female (95% CI)
Total	8.80% (8.36–9.27)	6.58% (6.07–7.12)	21.41% (20.81–22.03)
Army	9.75%* (9.01–10.53)	7.65%* (6.81–8.56)	22.87%* (21.92–23.84)
Navy	11.73%* (10.60–12.94)	8.34%* (7.02–9.81)	27.71%* (26.21–29.26)
Air Force	4.96%* (4.56–5.38)	3.26%* (2.80–3.77)	12.32%* (11.72–12.95)
Marines	7.68% (6.41–9.13)	6.11% (4.76–7.70)	27.19%* (24.68–29.80)

* Percentage is significantly different from the average of the other services within a column; p<.05, Bonferroni corrected.

however, we estimate that nearly one out of every eight women experienced such events in the past year. A more-detailed breakdown of the specific behaviors that constituted a *sexually hostile work environment* will be included in the full RAND report to be released in the spring of 2015.

These behaviors that respondents indicate are persistent or severe may have several negative effects. Case law demonstrates that a hostile work environment can cause poor work performance or evaluations, separation from the employer, and mental health problems. This type of harassment may also interfere with cohesion within military units, may degrade mission effectiveness, and may result in voluntary separations from service of qualified service members who find these behaviors to be an unacceptable condition of employment (Moore, 2010; Rosen, 1998; Sims, Drasgow, and Fitzgerald, 2005). Such events undermine the rights of service members, most often women, to fair treatment within the military. Careful tracking of this measure over time would provide a valuable gauge of progress in reducing sex-based violations of military equal opportunity.

The measure of *sexual quid pro quo* (a Latin phrase meaning "this for that") identifies incidents in which someone used his or her power or influence within the military to attempt to coerce sexual behavior. These events are counted in our measure only if the respondent indicated that they had personal evidence that a workplace benefit or punishment was contingent on a sexual behavior. Hearsay or rumor was not considered sufficient evidence to count in this category. Unlike *sexually hostile work environment*, this form of sexual harassment is comparatively rare (Table 6). We estimate with 95-percent confidence that approximately 1 in 60 women and 1 in 300 men

Table 6
Estimated Percentage of Active-Duty Service Members Who Experienced Sexual Quid Pro Quo in the Past Year, by Gender and Service Branch

Service	Total (95% CI)	Male (95% CI)	Female (95% CI)
Total	0.54% (0.41–0.70)	0.35% (0.21–0.55)	1.66% (1.46–1.89)
Army	0.65% (0.49–0.84)	0.41% (0.25–0.64)	2.12%* (1.79–2.49)
Navy	0.80% (0.43–1.38)	0.50% (0.12–1.34)	2.22% (1.70–2.85)
Air Force	0.14%* (0.10–0.20)	0.06%* (0.03–0.12)	0.50%* (0.37–0.65)
Marines	0.50% (0.16–1.20)	0.37% (0.05–1.26)	2.12% (1.31–3.25)

* Percentage is significantly different from the average of the other services within a column; p<.05, Bonferroni corrected.

were harassed this way in the past year. As with the other form of sexual harassment, members of the Air Force were at substantially lower risk for these events relative to the members of the other services.

Although *sexual quid pro quo* events are much rarer than those reflecting a *sexually hostile work environment,* they represent a particularly serious category of offense within the military. Because military leaders have a great deal of authority over service members' lives, more than supervisors in the civilian workplace, misuse of their authority is a significant concern. In some cases, these acts are also likely to be crimes (e.g., under UCMJ Article 133 and Article 134), not merely civil infractions. Thus, although rare, it may be valuable to monitor these offenses over time to assess the progress of military policies in reducing their prevalence.

The two measures of MEO violations that we have discussed thus far, *sexually hostile work environment* and *sexual quid pro quo,* together constitute the legal constructs describing sexual harassment. Thus, our sexual harassment measure (Table 7) counts anyone who has experienced either subtype of harassment. The overall measure of sexual harassment may not be as descriptively useful as its components, however, because it is dominated by the more common form of harassment (*sexually hostile work environment*). A comparison of Table 7 and Table 5 shows that the aggregate rate of *sexual harassment* is almost identical to the rate of *sexually hostile work environment*; this means that the vast majority of individuals who indicated they experienced a *sexual quid pro quo* also indicated being sexually harassed under *sexually hostile work environment*. This in turn suggests that sexually hostile work environments may put members at a higher risk for sexual quid pro quo overtures; that is, the vast majority of those

Table 7
Estimated Percentage of Active-Duty Service Members Who Experienced Sexual Harassment in the Past Year, By Gender and Service Branch

Service	Total (95% CI)	Male (95% CI)	Female (95% CI)
Total	8.85% (8.40–9.31)	6.61% (6.09–7.15)	21.57% (20.96–22.19)
Army	9.80%* (9.05–10.58)	7.67%* (6.83–8.58)	23.07%* (22.12–24.05)
Navy	11.78%* (10.65-12.99)	8.37%* (7.05–9.84)	27.82%* (26.31–29.36)
Air Force	4.99%* (4.60–5.42)	3.29%* (2.82–3.80)	12.43%* (11.82–13.07)
Marines	7.69% (6.42–9.14)	6.11% (4.76–7.70)	27.30%* (24.79–29.92)

* Percentage is significantly different from the average of the other services within a column; p<.05, Bonferroni corrected.

describing quid pro quo experiences also describe having experienced a sexually hostile workplace in the past year.[12]

The *gender discrimination* measure assesses incidents in which the respondent indicated that she or he was the recipient of derogatory comments or mistreatment on the basis of her or his gender. To count in this measure, respondents must indicate that the mistreatment also resulted in harm to their military career (i.e., adversely affect their evaluation, promotion, or assignment). We estimate that *gender discrimination* affected approximately one in eight women in the last year, but 1 in 60 men (Table 8). As with the harassment measure, women in the Air Force are estimated to be less than half as likely as those in other services to experience *gender discrimination* in the past year. Among men, our estimates suggest that both airmen and Marines experienced less *gender discrimination* relative to soldiers and sailors.

The concept of gender discrimination is particularly challenging to assess in a self-report survey. Unlike sexual harassment, many forms of gender discrimination occur without the victim's awareness. Because our estimates are based on self-reports, they cannot count incidents in which discrimination occurred without the respondent knowing. We cannot estimate how common these hidden cases of discrimination may be. On the other hand, respondents may sometimes attribute mistreatment to their gender when there are legitimately other causes of their adverse work experience.

In spite of these interpretational difficulties, the fact that one in every eight women perceived themselves to have been treated unfairly in the military because of their gender represents a significant problem. This perception may make it hard to retain women in the military (Defense Equal Opportunity Management Institute, 2008;

Table 8
Estimated Percentage of Active-Duty Service Members Who Experienced Gender Discrimination in the Past Year, by Gender and Service Branch

Service	Total (95% CI)	Male (95% CI)	Female (95% CI)
Total	3.33% (3.14–3.54)	1.73% (1.52–1.96)	12.40% (11.93–12.88)
Army	3.86%* (3.54–4.21)	2.11%* (1.77–2.49)	14.80%* (14.02–15.61)
Navy	4.65%* (4.07–5.28)	2.52%* (1.89–3.27)	14.65%* (13.50–15.86)
Air Force	1.95%* (1.78–2.13)	0.86%* (0.70–1.04)	6.69%* (6.23–7.17)
Marines	1.97%* (1.62–2.38)	0.87%* (0.60–1.23)	15.59%* (13.65–17.70)

* Percentage is significantly different from the average of the other services within a column; $p<.05$, Bonferroni corrected.

DMDC, 2009) and may make it less likely that women aspire to senior leadership roles (Hosek et al., 2001). To the extent that the broader public hears from women who believe they were treated unfairly in the military, it may affect the services' ability to recruit service members who put a high value on working in an equitable environment. Thus, perceptions about *gender discrimination* are an important target for intervention, and this measure should be valuable for assessing DoD policy and progress over time.

The three types of sex-based MEO violations (*sexually hostile work environment*, *sexual quid pro quo*, and *gender discrimination*) can be thought of as belonging to a broader construct: *any sex-based MEO violation* (Table 9). *Any sex-based MEO violation* totals are noticeably higher than the total for *sexually hostile work environment*, suggesting that many who indicated that they experienced *gender discrimination* did not also indicate experiencing a *sexually hostile work environment*. On the other hand, because this measure combines several distinct phenomena that are likely to be affected by different types of policy or educational interventions, this overall measure may not be ideal for evaluating DoD progress on achieving key MEO goals. Even relatively substantial changes in *gender discrimination* or *sexual quid pro quo* over time may be difficult to detect in this aggregate measure.

Table 9
Estimated Percentage of Active-Duty Service Members Who Experienced Any Sex-Based MEO Violation in the Past Year, by Gender and Service Branch

Service	Total (95% CI)	Male (95% CI)	Female (95% CI)
Total	10.21% (9.75–10.68)	7.43% (6.91–7.99)	25.97% (25.34–26.61)
Army	11.30%* (10.54–12.10)	8.53%* (7.67–9.45)	28.62%* (27.61–29.64)
Navy	13.56%* (12.39–14.79)	9.61%* (8.25–11.11)	32.16%* (30.62–33.72)
Air Force	6.05%* (5.64–6.48)	3.84%* (3.36–4.37)	15.66%* (14.99–16.35)
Marines	8.51%* (7.21–9.95)	6.65% (5.28–8.25)	31.43%* (28.85–34.11)

* Percentage is significantly different from the average of the other services within a column; p<.05, Bonferroni corrected.

Time Trends on Unwanted Sexual Contact and Sexual Harassment Measures

For historical purposes, we compare results from the portion of the 2014 survey fielded using the prior WGRA form to the earlier WGRA results collected using the same survey questions and analyzed using comparable methods. For reasons discussed later in this report, we believe the results from the WGRA survey questions are better thought of as measures of workplace climate with respect to unwanted gender-related behaviors (e.g., norms and culture) rather than counts of sex crimes or MEO violations per se; however, they serve as important indicators of change in climate over time.

Prior Form Unwanted Sexual Contact Results

Figure 1 illustrates trends in past-year unwanted sexual contact measured using the WGRA methodology.[13] In 2012, 6.1 percent of active-duty women were classified as having experienced unwanted sexual contact in the past year. In 2014 (Table 10), this number dropped to 4.3 percent, which is approximately the same as the percentage recorded in 2010 (4.4 percent) and significantly below the 2006 rate (6.8 percent).[14] Past-year unwanted sexual contact against men has not changed significantly over time, at 0.9 percent in 2014 compared with 1.2 percent in 2012, 0.9 percent in 2010, and 1.8 percent in 2006. Using the WGRA method for estimating past-year unwanted sexual contact in 2014, we can infer with 95-percent confidence that the total number of active-duty service members in the sample frame who experienced at least one unwanted sexual contact in the past year is between 16,000 and 22,000. Our best

Figure 1
Estimated Percentage of Active-Duty Service Men and Women Who Experienced Unwanted Sexual Contact in the Past Year, as Defined by the WGRA Methodology, 2006–2014

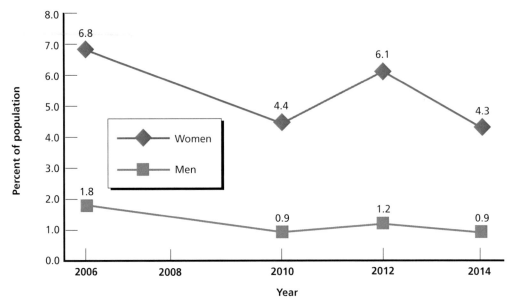

Note: 2006 estimates are for calendar year 2006. Estimates for 2010, 2012, and 2014 are for a time period closer to the fiscal year.

Table 10
Estimated Percentage of Active-Duty Service Members Who Experienced Unwanted Sexual Contact in the Past Year, by Gender and Service Branch

Service	Total (95% CI)	Male (95% CI)	Female (95% CI)
Total	1.43% (1.23–1.66)	0.93% (0.71–1.20)	4.31% (3.89–4.76)
Army	1.70% (1.29–2.19)	1.24% (0.80–1.83)	4.59% (3.90–5.37)
Navy	1.79% (1.37–2.30)	1.08% (0.64–1.71)	5.11% (4.15–6.21)
Air Force	0.78%* (0.62–0.97)	0.43%* (0.26–0.66)	2.28%* (1.89–2.72)
Marines	1.23% (0.81–1.80)	0.66% (0.28–1.31)	8.44%* (6.28-11.05)

* Percentage is significantly different than average of the other services within column; p<.05, Bonferroni corrected.

estimate in this range is that approximately 19,000 active-duty service members experienced unwanted sexual contact in the past year, out of 1,317,561 active-duty members.

In 2014, we estimate that Marine Corps women experienced past-year unwanted sexual contact at rates that are significantly higher than women from other services, as was also found in 2012. Similarly, as in 2012, members of the Air Force, both men and women, are estimated to have significantly lower rates of past-year unwanted sexual contact than their peers in other services.

Changes in the prevalence of unwanted sexual contact over time were also investigated within each branch of service. Among men, the 2014 rates are not statistically significantly lower than 2012, 2010, or 2006 rates for any service except for the Navy, which has a 2014 rate significantly lower than in 2012. Similarly, among women, these declines were not always statistically significant. For active-duty women in the Army, 2014 estimated rates of unwanted sexual contact are lower than in 2012 and 2006, but not significantly lower than in 2010. For women in the Navy, estimated rates of unwanted sexual contact in the past year are significantly lower in 2014 than in 2012, but not significantly lower than was found in 2010 or 2006. For women in the Air Force, 2014 rates are lower than in 2006, but not significantly lower than in 2012 or 2010. For active-duty Marine Corps women, 2014 rates of unwanted sexual contact are not significantly lower than in any of the prior years (2012, 2010, or 2006).

Because some service members may have experienced more than one unwanted sexual contact in the past year, prior form respondents were asked to provide details on what happened during the "one event that had the greatest effect on you." Table 11 displays the distribution of types of unwanted sexual contact described as occurring in that "one event" among those respondents who experienced an unwanted sexual contact in the past year. The proportion of events involving sexual touching only, attempted penetrative assault, and completed penetrative assault are not significantly different from the same proportions reported in 2012, when 32.5 percent of all women classified

Table 11
Type of Unwanted Sexual Contact in Event That Had the Greatest Effect on the Service Member, by Gender

	Total (95% CI)	Male (95% CI)	Female (95% CI)
Unwanted sexual touching (only)	40.67% (33.04–48.64)	49.38% (36.22–62.60)	30.03% (25.48–34.89)
Attempted sexual intercourse, anal or oral sex	20.33% (15.89–25.37)	11.47% (5.81–19.72)	31.14% (26.40–36.18)
Completed sexual intercourse, anal or oral sex	19.26% (14.97–24.16)	11.45% (5.91–19.46)	28.80% (24.19–33.76)
None of the above	19.75% (13.05–27.99)	27.70% (16.28–41.73)	10.03% (7.14–13.61)

as experiencing unwanted sexual contact indicated that the worst event consisted of sexual touching only, without penetration or attempted penetration; 26.4 percent indicated that it was attempted sexual intercourse, anal sex, or oral sex; and 31.4 percent indicated that it was completed sexual intercourse, anal sex, or oral sex. The percentage of men estimated to have experienced unwanted sexual contact also saw no significant changes between 2012 and 2014 in the distribution of types of contact experienced during the one event that had the "greatest effect." In 2012, 50.7 percent of men indicating a past-year unwanted sexual contact were classified as having a "one event" that involved sexual touching only; 5.2 percent involved attempted sexual intercourse, anal sex, or oral sex; and 9.8 percent involved completed sexual intercourse, anal sex, or oral sex.

As in 2012, a surprisingly large percentage of men classified as having experienced unwanted sexual contact indicated that none of the component behaviors that define unwanted sexual contact occurred in the "one event" that had the greatest effect (27.7 percent in 2014, 34.3 percent in 2012). This lack of specificity was not due to respondents skipping these questions. Rather, 74 percent of respondents in the "none of the above" category answered every question but indicated that each of the behaviors listed did not occur. This suggests that either (a) these individuals were incorrectly identified as having experienced an unwanted sexual contact in the past year or (b) that they did have an unwanted sexual contact in the past year, but chose as their "one event" an incident that was not an unwanted sexual contact. In either case, it appears that the series of questions about the "one event" may include a substantial number of people who responded about incidents that do not qualify as criminal assaults.

The WGRA form contained items assessing possible retaliation against those respondents who reported an unwanted sexual contact to military authorities in the past year. SAPRO requested that we provide estimates on these retaliation items in this top-line report because retaliation is a measure used by DoD to track progress in its efforts to reduce stigma associated with reporting sexual assaults. The WGRA form contains items assessing possible retaliation against those respondents who reported an unwanted sexual contact to military authorities in the past year. These items ask respondents if they have experienced any retaliation or punishment as a result of the one event that had the greatest effect on them, including professional retaliation (such as being denied promotion or training), social retaliation (such as being ignored by coworkers), adverse administrative actions (such as being transferred to a different assignment), or punishments for violations associated with the event (such as for underage drinking). In the WGRA portion of our 2014 study, 62 percent of women who reported an unwanted sexual contact to military authorities indicated that they experienced at least one form of retaliation (with a 95-percent confidence interval of 51 percent to 72 percent). This is similar to what was found in 2012, when 62 percent of women indicated they experienced at least one form of retaliation. (Reliable estimates could not be estimated for males indicating harassment after reporting an unwanted sexual contact in neither the 2012 nor the 2014 survey). Among this number:

- 32 percent indicated that they experienced professional retaliation (95-percent confidence interval: 23 percent to 42 percent)
- 53 percent indicated that they experienced social retaliation (95-percent confidence interval: 42 percent to 63 percent)
- 35 percent indicated that they experienced adverse actions (95-percent confidence interval: 25 percent to 45 percent)
- 11 percent indicated that they experienced punishments (95-percent confidence interval: 5 percent to 18 percent).

Prior Form Sexual Harassment Results

Estimates of the percentage of service members who experienced sexual harassment in the past year measured in 2014 using WGRA definitions are shown in Table 12; Figure 2 places these estimates in the context of the previous surveys. These estimates suggest that fewer active-duty women in 2014 were sexually harassed in the past year than in 2012. Indeed, the estimated 20.2 percent of service women who experienced sexual harassment in the past year was 3 percentage points lower than in 2012 and 12.5 percentage points lower than in 2006. The share of service men who were classified as having experienced sexual harassment in the past year in 2014 (3.5 percent) and 2012 (4.1 percent) did not differ significantly. However, the 2.5 percentage point decrease between 2006 and 2014 represents a significant reduction among service men that were classified as having experienced sexual harassment in the past year.

Table 12
Estimated Percentage of Active-Duty Service Members in 2014 Who Experienced Sexual Harassment as Measured in the WGRA in the Past Year, by Gender and Service Branch

Service	Total (95% CI)	Male (95% CI)	Female (95% CI)
Total	6.00% (5.61–6.41)	3.50% (3.07–3.97)	20.23% (19.45–21.03)
Army	6.83%* (6.15–7.57)	4.29%* (3.54–5.13)	22.74%* (21.40–24.12)
Navy	7.69%* (6.78–8.69)	4.54% (3.55–5.73)	22.48%* (20.68–24.36)
Air Force	4.03%* (3.67–4.42)	1.65%* (1.32–2.03)	14.31%* (13.38–15.28)
Marines	4.27%* (3.14–5.65)	2.68% (1.56–4.28)	24.11% (20.89–27.57)

* Percentage is significantly different than average of the other services within column; p<.05, Bonferroni corrected.

Figure 2
Estimated Percentages of Active-Duty Men and Women Who Experienced Sexual Harassment in the Past Year, as Defined by the WGRA Methodology, 2006–2014

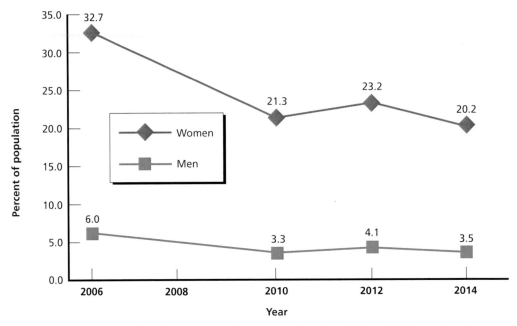

Note: 2006 estimates are for calendar year 2006. Estimates for 2010, 2012, and 2014 are for a time period closer to the fiscal year.

Across the four services, we estimate that Air Force men and women were less likely to experience sexual harassment relative to members in other services in 2014. A comparison over time for service-specific estimates indicates that women in the Army experienced a significantly lower rate of sexual harassment in 2014 compared with 2012, 2010, and 2006. Women in the Air Force experienced a significantly higher rate of past-year sexual harassment in 2014 compared with 2010, a lower rate compared with 2006, but no significant difference relative to 2012. Women in the Navy saw a significant decrease compared with 2006, but no significant changes since then. Women in the Marines are estimated to have significantly lower rates of sexual harassment in 2014 compared with 2012 and 2006, but this rate is not statistically different than the 2010 rates. Among men, service-specific percentages of past-year sexual harassment were not significantly different from 2012. Active-duty men in the Navy, Army, and Air Force all have significantly lower estimated rates of past-year sexual harassment in 2014 than were observed in 2006, but current rates are not significantly lower than in 2012 or 2010. The sexual harassment rate for men in the Marines has not declined significantly compared with rates measured in any of these prior surveys (2012, 2010, or 2006).

Comparing Results Across the Two Survey Instruments

Results using the WGRA questions and methods are included in this report for historical comparisons and to establish a link between our new measures of sexual assault and sexual harassment and the time trends for unwanted gender-related behaviors as they have been measured up to 2014. However, this portion of the study also allows for a direct comparison between the prior method of counting unwanted sexual contact and sexual harassment and the methods developed specifically for the RMWS.

Although top-line rates of exposure to sexual assault (or, under the WGRA, unwanted sexual contact) and sexual harassment as measured by the WGRA and RMWS are similar, this apparent similarity conceals large differences in the people counted and the types of crimes they experienced. The RMWS was designed to capture sex crimes as defined in the UCMJ and MEO violations as defined in the UCMJ and other law. In contrast, the WGRA measures a climate of unwanted sexual experiences associated with illegal behavior, but was not designed as a precise crime measure. As summarized below, the WGRA counts some people who have not experienced sex crimes or MEO violations in the past year, while at the same time missing others who have had such experiences. The fact that these over- and undercounts approximately cancel one another out should not be taken as evidence that the WGRA questionnaire offers a satisfactory measure of sexual offenses for purposes of tracking the effectiveness of DoD policies or for estimating the total number of offenses occurring against service men and women. Measures that do not accurately and precisely count those people or events that are the target of training, prevention, or other policies or programs are unlikely to be sensitive to changes brought about by these programs. For example, the implementation of policies that effectively reduce sexual assaults may not result in a detectable corresponding change in this measure of unwanted sexual contact.

We summarize here some of the key differences in the offenses counted by the two methods. A more complete discussion of these differences will be included in RAND's final report, available in the spring of 2015.

1. **Approximately 25 percent of self-identified past-year unwanted sexual contact events described on the WGRA as the one event having the greatest effect on the respondent did not occur within the past year.** Both the WGRA and the RMWS questionnaires ask about events occurring in the past year. Prior research shows that many respondents report crimes as having taken place in the past year when they actually experienced them more than a year ago. This kind of timeframe "telescoping" can lead to substantially overestimated crime rates (Andersen, Frankel, and Kasper, 1979; Cantor, 1989; Lehnen & Skogan, 1984). To minimize this bias, the RMWS incorporated many techniques designed to reduce or limit response telescoping. This appears to have been effective. At the end of the sexual assault section on the RMWS survey and the end of the

"unwanted sexual contact" section on the prior WGRA form, we asked respondents to confirm that the event they were describing occurred in the past year.[15] Whereas 7 percent taking the RMWS said they were sure the event actually occurred more than a year ago (i.e., should not be counted as a past-year event), 25 percent of prior form respondents said they were sure the event occurred more than a year ago. More importantly, in the RMWS survey, respondents who confirmed that their sexual assaults occurred more than one year ago were excluded from the past-year estimates. Using the standard WGRA procedures, the much larger portion who acknowledged errors in their timing of the event were nevertheless included in estimates for the rate of past year unwanted sexual contact, which results in overcounting.

2. **If treated as a crime measure, the WGRA substantially undercounts criminal penetrative assaults.** The WGRA cannot accurately estimate the number of penetrative sexual assaults experienced by service members in the past year. The only description detailing types of assault occurs for the event described by respondents as the one having the "greatest effect" on them during the past year. This may or may not reflect the distribution of penetrative assaults among all the unwanted sexual contact experiences reported by service members. Estimates for 2014 using the WGRA methods suggest there were approximately 3,500 (with a 95-percent confidence interval of 2,900 to 4,600) penetrative assaults among these "greatest effect" contacts in the past year (including those that were improperly included due to the telescoping problem described above). In contrast, the RMWS measure assesses whether any of the sexual assaults experienced by the service member in the past year could be counted as a penetrative assault. This estimate suggests the number of penetrative assaults is more than twice as large, or 8,000 (with a 95-percent confidence interval of 6,500 to 9,400), as was measured under the WGRA. This effect is most pronounced among men, with the WGRA methods yielding estimates that are less than one-third the rate found using the RMWS measures (1,000 versus 3,500, with 95-percent confidence intervals of 600 to 2,100 and 2,400 to 5,300, respectively). There may be several reasons for this discrepancy, most notably the survey questions themselves. The RMWS survey asks three specific and detailed questions about penetrative sexual assault that align closely with the definitions used in the UCMJ; those three questions are asked of everyone in the survey. In contrast, the WGRA first filters out most respondents on the basis of a single complex gating question. Then, among the remainder, it only asks about the type of unwanted sexual contact during the "one event" selected by the respondent. The series of questions used to determine type of unwanted sexual contact lacks definitions of key terms, and the wording does not align closely with specific behavioral definitions in the UCMJ.

3. **The unwanted sexual contact measure from the WGRA may count many events that are not crimes as defined by the UCMJ.** A large percentage of respondents on the WGRA indicate that their unwanted sexual contact is not described by any of the options meant to classify sexual assaults. In responses to the prior (WGRA) form, for instance, 14.6 percent of those classified as having experienced an unwanted sexual contact say the "one event" did not involve another person doing any of the behaviors defining unwanted sexual contact: sexually touching; attempting unsuccessfully to have sexual intercourse; making the respondent have sexual intercourse; attempting unsuccessfully to make the respondent perform or receive oral sex, anal sex, or penetration by a finger or object; or making the respondent perform or receive oral sex, anal sex, or penetration by a finger or object.[16] In other words, many respondents who are classified as experiencing an unwanted sexual contact selected as their "one event" an incident that does not match any of the criteria defining an unwanted sexual contact.

One of the criticisms of the WGRA measure has been that it does not distinguish experiences that were criminal, as opposed to merely unwanted (Schenck, 2014). While such a distinction was, according to the WGRA survey developers, never the goal of the unwanted sexual contact measure, considerable confusion arose over how the unwanted sexual contact results should be interpreted. The more-detailed assessment provided by the RMWS survey applies the definitional criteria contained in UCMJ Article 120 to rule out noncriminal events. The 2014 prior form (WGRA) estimates suggest there were approximately 15,500 service members who experienced an unwanted sexual contact that did not involve penetration described as the one event having the "greatest effect" on respondents during the past year (called either *unwanted sexual touching, unwanted attempted sex,* or *none of the above* on the question asking about the type of assault). In contrast, the RMWS identified 13,000 cases of non-penetrative crimes in the past year. Thus, it may be that the RWMS is excluding from its count people who would have been counted as having experienced an unwanted sexual contact on the WGRA, but whose experience does not meet the legal threshold for a sexual assault. Alternatively, it is possible that a large number of WGRA respondents who had experienced a penetrative sexual assault in the past year chose instead to describe a separate non-penetrative sexual assault as the one event having the greatest effect on them. We plan further analyses to better distinguish these possibilities and to better document the differences between the two measures.

Implications of the Top-Line Results

Our findings from the portion of our study conducted using the prior WGRA form suggest that unwanted sexual contact and sexual harassment, as these have been measured over the past eight years, have declined for active-duty women since 2012, but they are not significantly lower than the percentages observed in 2010. Similarly, a smaller percentage of men are experiencing past-year unwanted sexual contacts or sexual harassment today than in 2006, though most of the change in these trends occurred between 2006 and 2010. Since then, the percentage of men reporting past-year unwanted sexual contact or sexual harassment has remained steady at around 1 percent and 3–4 percent, respectively.

Together, these trend data suggest that fewer unwanted sexual contacts are occurring in the military than was the case just two years ago and in 2006, but significant improvements over 2010 levels have not occurred.

Whereas these trend data offer useful information about aspects of the workplace climate that are associated with sexual offenses and whether or not this climate is improving, they do not provide reliable information on the number of actual criminal sexual assaults and sex-based MEO violations that occur against service members annually. These are, however, what the new RMWS survey was designed to measure.

Our estimates suggest that between 18,000 and 22,500 active-duty service members were sexually assaulted in the past year, or approximately 1 percent of all service men and 5 percent of service women. These are one-year rates, so over a several-year career, the percentage of service members who have experienced at least one sexual assault will necessarily be higher. It is also important to note that these figures are not a count of sexual assaults, but rather of service members who indicated that they experienced one or more sexual assaults. The actual number of sexual assaults in the past year is necessarily higher. It is equally important to recognize that the perpetrators of these assaults may be military service members or civilians, and in some cases the military status of the perpetrator is unknown. Moreover, the nature of these assaults appears to be different than previously thought: 43 percent of assaulted women and 35 percent of assaulted men are classified as having experienced a *penetrative sexual assault*. In contrast, the results we obtained for 2014 using the WGRA measures suggest that among individuals who indicated an unwanted sexual contact, 29 percent of women and 11 percent of men experienced an event that included penetration. That is, the RMWS measure identifies more penetrative assaults against women and substantially more penetrative assaults against men than the WGRA measure.

Another important finding is the high rate of sex-based MEO violations against active-duty service women. We estimate that more than a quarter of active-duty women experienced a sex-based MEO violation in the past year, the vast majority of which involve having to work in a sexually hostile environment. Among women in the Navy and Marines, the rate approaches one-third of all service members. By definition, these experiences are unwanted, and they are offensive, humiliating, and they interfere with women's equitable treatment in the workplace. At such high rates, sexual harassment and other MEO violations could affect cohesion within military units, degrade mission effectiveness, and result in voluntary separations from service of qualified service members who find these behaviors to be an unacceptable condition of employment (Moore, 2010; Rosen, 1998; Sims, Drasgow, and Fitzgerald, 2005).

Although we estimate that a lower percentage of men than women experienced MEO violations in the past year, our estimates are considerably larger than rates of sexual harassment of men found using the WGRA methods, and they are high enough to merit attention. In the Navy, for instance, we estimate that 1 in 10 men experienced sex-based MEO violations in the past year. In the Army, it is almost 1 in 12. For men, the largest source of problems stems from having experienced a sexually hostile work environment, which generally reflects an inappropriately sexualized workplace that they have found to be offensive. Among women, however, both gender discrimination and having experienced a sexually hostile work environment were common types of MEO violations. We have much to learn from more-detailed analyses of the survey results about the context of these crimes and MEO violations—for example, who in the workplace is committing them and where they are occurring. This more-detailed analysis will be included in our forthcoming final report.

Some will ask how these numbers compare to what would be found in similar civilian populations, perhaps on college campuses or in law enforcement or emergency management agencies. Credible comparisons are difficult to make, however, because of demographic and other differences between military populations and civilian populations. Rates of sexual assault are likely to be sensitive to the age distribution in the population, the gender balance, education levels, the proportions that are married, duty hours, sleeping accommodations, alcohol availability, and many other sexual-assault risk factors that differ between the active-duty population and various candidate comparison groups.

Better comparisons may be possible between different military components. For instance, our study finds that men and women in the Air Force experience lower rates of sexual assault and sex-based MEO violations than members of other services. Such differences raise important questions about whether these differences are attributable to policy or cultural factors, or whether they may be explained by known differences in the demographic makeup of each service, including factors such as age, education level, marital status, and seniority. By analyzing these and other differences, we expect to be able to learn more about the factors that contribute to better or worse outcomes. The forthcoming final RAND report will include detailed analyses investigating these questions, including the extent to which differences in age, gender, education, or occupational roles explain the differences in observed rates of sexual assault and sex-based MEO violations across services.

As with all survey research, the results presented here are subject to several types of measurement error. While we have taken steps to minimize the likelihood of these errors, there is no way to completely eliminate them. As noted before, a thorough forensic investigation would likely discover that some of the events identified as crimes really were not crimes, and that some events not counted as crimes were. Moreover, it is possible that the individuals who did not respond to the survey have either higher or lower rate of sexual assaults than those who did respond, even after applying analytic weights designed to minimize those differences. We are conducting ongoing research, including additional data collection among service members who did not respond to this survey, to better quantify the likelihood and direction of any such errors.

Also, because we omitted service members with less than six months of service from our sample, we have not counted some portion of service members who experienced sexual assaults or harassment in their first months in the military. On the other hand, some in our sample with between 6 and 12 months of service have been counted as experiencing one of these events even though it may have occurred a few months before they entered active-duty service. Again, in later reports, we will explore the timing of these events.

The 2014 RMWS survey was designed to address some of the criticisms made of 2012 WGRA and prior versions of that survey, and to make the focus of the survey more clearly on crimes under the UCMJ and violations of equal opportunity laws and regulations. The RMWS had many more respondents, a higher response rate, and an analytic sample that is representative of the population on a wider set of character-istics that are risk factors for sexual assault or harassment. The new RMWS survey instrument collects more-detailed information about these events, uses simpler ques-tions, more clearly restricts the questions to events that occurred in the past year, and excludes events that do not meet the legal standards for sexual assault, sexual harass-ment, or gender discrimination. In spite of these improvements, the RMWS has con-firmed some of the core findings of the earlier WGRA surveys. In particular, several policymakers and critics have expressed concern that the actual rate of sex offenses in the military was being overstated by imprecise estimates provided by the *unwanted sexual contact* question—suggesting that the top-line numbers included many minor, or even accidental, physical contacts. Our estimates suggest that the prior WGRA measures and methods actually *underestimate* the proportion of service members who experienced at least one penetrative sex offense in the past year. However, our study also shows that the percentage who experienced a past-year sex offense has declined over the past two years within the population of active-duty DoD service members to levels similar to those observed in 2010.

Next Steps

This report describes only the preliminary top-line findings from the RMWS. These top-line results are likely to generate many questions about the details of the sexual assaults and sex-based MEO violations that we have documented here, as well as about differences in estimates produced by the prior WGRA form and the new RMWS questionnaire. The RAND team will analyze these and other topics through the winter of 2014–2015, and we will provide these more-detailed analyses, along with public reports on the methodology and the main findings, in the late spring of 2015. These reports will include findings on

- rates of past-year sexual assault, sexual harassment, and gender discrimination among
  - DoD active-duty and reserve-component members
  - Coast Guard active-duty and reserve-component members
- service members' experiences with support and prosecution systems available to those who report sexual assaults or MEO violations
- contextual and risk factors associated with sexual assaults and MEO violations
- results from investigations designed to understand the reliability and validity of our survey estimates
- recommendations for future surveys of sexual assault and sexual harassment in the military.

Appendix: A Brief Overview of RMWS Weighting Procedures

Respondent data were weighted to ensure that our analytic sample was representative of the active-duty population on key characteristics. Such weights are standard with all professional survey research to reduce bias in the survey estimates (Little and Rubin, 2002; Schafer and Graham 2002). Two sets of weights are used in this report. When presenting 2014 results from the prior WGRA form items, we use the weighting procedures that were used in 2012 (see details in DMDC, 2012). These weights are designed primarily to ensure a representative analytic sample on gender, branch of service, pay grade, and minority status (e.g., the analytic sample contains the correct proportion of female Marines who are junior enlisted minorities). The weights also consider family status, deployment status, and combat occupation, but do not achieve exact balance on those factors.

When presenting results for the new assessments from the RMWS forms, we used weights designed to make the analytic sample representative on a broader range of factors than were used in the 2012 analyses. These additional factors take into account information about socio-demographic characteristics (e.g., age, race), occupation (e.g., respondent's occupation code, percent of respondent's occupation code that is male, deployment history, time served in the military), and survey fieldwork measures (e.g., missing email address, missing mail address, number of letters returned as undeliverable, percentage of emails that were returned as undeliverable). Using either the 2012 WGRA weighting method or the RMWS weighting method, the distribution of the weighted respondents matches the full DoD population across the key reporting categories of gender, branch of service, and pay grade (see Table A.1). The weights used on the new RMWS assessments, however, further balance the sample within each reporting category on those key variables associated with sexual assault, sexual harassment, and gender discrimination. To the extent that these key variables are also associated with whether service members respond to the survey, this approach reduces nonresponse bias in the population estimates of sexual assault, sexual harassment, or gender discrimination.

Data analyses included estimation of outcomes across all respondent samples and for the different reporting categories. For categorical variables, weighted percentages and standard errors were computed with SAS PROC SURVEYFREQ. The variance of weighted estimates was calculated using the Taylor series method. These analyses were conducted in SAS version 9.3. Comparison of weighted proportions across two groups (e.g., comparing an estimate from the 2014 prior form to the 2012 WGRA) were done using tests that appropriately accounted for the survey weighting in computing point estimates and respective standard errors. To control the familywise error rate, some significance tests apply a Bonferroni correction for multiple testing. Specifically, we ensured that the familywise error rate for each gender by services table, containing six independent hypothesis tests, is below .05. When providing counts of individuals in the population, this report rounds to the nearest 500 to avoid implying greater precision than actually exists for these estimates.

Table A.1
Balance of Weighted Respondents to the Full DoD Population, by Weight Type

Reporting Category	Population N	Population Percentage	Sample Percent WGRS Weights	Sample Percent RMWS Weights
Female, Air Force, Junior Enlisted	20,063	1.52%	1.52%	1.52%
Female, Air Force, Junior Officer	8,065	0.61%	0.61%	0.61%
Female, Air Force, Senior Enlisted	26,826	2.04%	2.04%	2.04%
Female, Air Force, Senior Officer	4,370	0.33%	0.33%	0.33%
Female, Army, Junior Enlisted	30,960	2.35%	2.35%	2.35%
Female, Army, Junior Officer	9,711	0.74%	0.74%	0.74%
Female, Army, Senior Enlisted	24,099	1.83%	1.83%	1.83%
Female, Army, Senior Officer	4,675	0.35%	0.35%	0.35%
Female, Marine, Junior Enlisted	8,709	0.66%	0.66%	0.66%
Female, Marine, Junior Officer	990	0.08%	0.08%	0.08%
Female, Marine, Senior Enlisted	3,795	0.29%	0.29%	0.29%
Female, Marine, Senior Officer	282	0.02%	0.02%	0.02%
Female, Navy, Junior Enlisted	27,613	2.10%	2.10%	2.10%
Female, Navy, Junior Officer	5,989	0.45%	0.45%	0.45%
Female, Navy, Senior Enlisted	18,630	1.41%	1.41%	1.41%
Female, Navy, Senior Officer	2,714	0.21%	0.21%	0.21%
Male, Air Force, Junior Enlisted	91,740	6.96%	6.96%	6.96%
Male, Air Force, Junior Officer	26,971	2.05%	2.05%	2.05%

Table A.1—Continued

Reporting Category	Population N	Population Percentage	Sample Percent WGRS Weights	Sample Percent RMWS Weights
Male, Air Force, Senior Enlisted	113,243	8.59%	8.59%	8.59%
Male, Air Force, Senior Officer	23,504	1.78%	1.78%	1.78%
Male, Army, Junior Enlisted	183,363	13.92%	13.92%	13.92%
Male, Army, Junior Officer	39,708	3.01%	3.01%	3.01%
Male, Army, Senior Enlisted	183,498	13.93%	13.93%	13.93%
Male, Army, Senior Officer	27,069	2.05%	2.05%	2.05%
Male, Marine, Junior Enlisted	101,800	7.73%	7.73%	7.73%
Male, Marine, Junior Officer	11,369	0.86%	0.86%	0.86%
Male, Marine, Senior Enlisted	53,295	4.04%	4.04%	4.04%
Male, Marine, Senior Officer	6,270	0.48%	0.48%	0.48%
Male, Navy, Junior Enlisted	98,531	7.48%	7.48%	7.48%
Male, Navy, Junior Officer	24,578	1.87%	1.87%	1.87%
Male, Navy, Senior Enlisted	117,396	8.91%	8.91%	8.91%
Male, Navy, Senior Officer	17,735	1.35%	1.35%	1.35%
TOTAL	**1,317,561**			

NOTES: WRGA weights refer to the system of sample weights used for the estimates based on the prior form survey. RMWS weights refer to the system used on estimates from the RAND forms. *Junior Enlisted* includes personnel in pay grades E-1 through E-4. *Senior Enlisted* includes personnel in pay grades E-5 through E-9 and W-1 through W-5 (warrant officers). *Junior Officer* includes personnel in pay grades O-1 through O-3, and *Senior Officer* includes personnel in pay grades O-4 through O-6.

References

Andersen, Roland, Martin R. Frankel, and Judith Kasper, *Total Survey Error: Applications to Improve Health Surveys*, San Francisco: Jossey-Bass Publishers, 1979, pp. 19–20, 32–37, 42–50, 52–74.

Cantor, David, "Substantive Implications of Longitudinal Design Features: The National Crime Survey As a Case Study," in D. Kasprzyk, G. Duncan, G. Kalton, & M. P. Singh (Eds.), *Panel Surveys*, New York: John Wiley, 1989, pp. 25–51.

Defense Equal Opportunity Management Institute, Directorate of Research, *Defense Equal Opportunity Climate Survey (DEOCS)*, 2008.

Defense Manpower Data Center, "November 2008 Status of Forces Survey of Active Duty Members: Administration, Datasets, and Codebook," Report No. 2008-033, 2009.

———, *2012 Workplace and Gender Relations Survey of Active Duty Members: Statistical Methodology Report*, DMDC Report No. 2012-067, December 2012.

Hosek, Susan D., Peter Tiemeyer, M. Rebecca Kilburn, Debra A. Strong, Selika Ducksworth, and Reginald Ray, *Minority and Gender Differences in Officer Career Progression*, Santa Monica, Calif.: RAND Corporation, MR-1184-OSD, 2001. As of October 24, 2014: http://www.rand.org/pubs/monograph_reports/MR1184.html

Lehnen, Robert.G., and Wesley G. Skogan (eds), *The National Crime Survey: Working Papers; Volume II: Methodological Studies*, U.S. Department of Justice, Bureau of Justice Statistics NCJ-90307, October 1984.

Little, Roderick J. A., and Donald B. Rubin, *Statistical Analysis With Missing Data* (2nd ed.), New York: Wiley-Interscience, 2002.

McMahon, Brian, and Thomas Feger Pugh, *Epidemiology: Principles and Methods*, Boston, Mass.: Little, Brown & Company, 1970.

Moore, Brenda L., *Effects of Sexual Harassment on Job Satisfaction, Retention, Cohesion, Commitment and Unit Effectiveness*, Defense Equal Opportunity Management Institute Directorate of Research, Technical Report (Executive Summary) # 08-10, 2010.

National Research Council, *Estimating the Incidence of Rape and Sexual Assault*, Candace Kruttschnitt, William D. Kalsbeek, and Carol C. House (eds.), Washington, D.C.: The National Academies Press, 2014.

Office of Management and Budget, *Standards and Guidelines for Statistical Surveys*, Washington, D.C., 2006. As of October 3, 2014: http://www.whitehouse.gov/sites/default/files/omb/inforeg/statpolicy/standards_stat_surveys.pdf

Rosen, Leora N., "Sexual Harassment, Cohesion and Combat Readiness in U.S. Army Support Units," *Armed Forces and Society*, Winter, 1998, Vol. 24, pp. 221–244.

Schafer, Joseph L., and John W. Graham, "Missing Data: Our View of the State of the Art," *Psychological Methods*, Vol. 7, No. 2, 2002, pp. 147–177.

Schenck, Lisa, "Testimony Before the Response Systems to Adult Sexual Assault Crimes Panel (RSP)," *Public Meeting of the Response Systems to Adult Sexual Assault Crimes Panel*, May 5–6, 2014. As of October 28, 2014:
http://responsesystemspanel.whs.mil/index.php/meetings/meetings-panel-sessions/20130505-06

Sims, Carra S., Fritz Drasgow, and Louise F. Fitzgerald, "The Effects of Sexual Harassment on Turnover in the Military: Time-Dependent Modeling, *Journal of Applied Psychology*, Vol. 90, No. 6, November 2005, pp. 1141–1152.

U.S. Department of Defense, "Department of Defense Military Equal Opportunity (MEO) Program," DoD Directive 1350.2, August 18, 1995, incorporating Change 1, May 7, 1997, certified current as of November 21, 2003.

Notes

[1] DoD Directive 1350.2 defines military equal opportunity (MEO) violations with respect to sex and other protected characteristics, and the survey questions closely align with these definitions. However, this DoD Directive is based on federal civil rights laws (e.g., Title VII of the Civil Rights Act of 1964). One difference between MEO and the federal definitions of equal employment opportunity violations is that MEO defines all persistent or severe harassment based on sex as an unfair condition of military employment.

[2] The Coast Guard results will be reported separately.

[3] Multiple versions of the RAND form were used to minimize respondent burden and costs to the services. It is not necessary to collect general experiences and attitudes from the entire sample in order to derive precise results, and doing so would be wasteful of service members' time. Therefore, we designed the survey so that each question was posed to only as many service members as was necessary to provide the needed precision required for the question. In general, those items that are endorsed relatively rarely (such as past year sexual assault) must be asked of the largest number of people to arrive at precise estimates, whereas items endorsed by large numbers (such as attitudinal questions), need only be asked of a comparatively small sample.

Thus, all sampled members were randomly assigned to receive one of four forms:

1. A "long form" consisting of a sexual assault module; a sex-based MEO violation module, which assesses sexual harassment and gender discrimination; and questions on respondent demographics, psychological state, command climate, attitudes, and beliefs about sexual assault in the military and the nation, and other related issues.
2. A "medium form" consisting of the sexual assault module, the sex-based MEO violation module, and some demographic questions.
3. A "short form" consisting of the full sexual assault module, the screening items only from the sex-based MEO violation module, and demographic questions. Thus, these respondents did not complete the full, sex-based MEO violation assessment.
4. The "prior WGRA form," which included questions from the 2012 WGRA, including the unwanted sexual contact, sexual harassment, and gender discrimination assessments from that survey.

[4] These figures include only DoD active-duty forces. They exclude the U.S. Coast Guard active-duty sample, which will be described in a separate report.

[5] Assignment to different conditions was not done with equal probability across survey types. Instead, we selected samples of approximately 100,000 for the prior WGRA form and 377,500 to complete one of the three RAND forms (60,000 long form, 159,000 medium form, and 159,000 short form).

[6] RAND's Institutional Review Board reviewed and approved the study procedures and survey instrument to ensure that it met all human subjects' protection protocols. The Office of the Under Secretary of Defense for Personnel and Readiness (OUSD/P&R) and the Coast Guard's Institutional Review Board both conducted second-level review of human subjects' protections. The study procedures, or portions of them, also received reviews and approvals by the OSD Office of General Counsel, the Chief Privacy Officer of OSD and the Joint Staff, the Defense Manpower Data Center (DMDC) Chief Privacy Officer, OUSD/P&R Records management, and the Joint Chiefs of Staff. The project received licensing approval from the Washington Headquarters Service after receiving approvals from the OUSD/P&R. In addition, we solicited multiple rounds of reviews and comments with our scientific review board and from researchers and leadership from each service's sexual assault prevention and response office.

[7] Our calculation of the 30.4 percent DoD active-duty response rate uses the most conservative of the American Association of Public Opinion Research definitions of response rates (RR1). If Coast Guard active-duty members are included, the RR1 was 31.0 percent. The design-weighted versions of the RR1 metric are 28.8 percent and 29.8 percent for the active-duty sample, excluding and including USCG active-duty members, respectively (more information on weighting procedures and on the distribution of the weighted respondents is included in the appendix to this volume). Because respondents completed different forms, the total number of responses on each of the key survey modules varied as follows:

Number of Active-Duty DoD Respondents Who Completed Each Survey Module

Survey Module	Sample Size	Respondents	Response Rate
WGRA Outcomes (prior form)	100,000	29,541	29.5%
RMWS Sexual Assault Outcomes	377,513	115,759	30.7%
RMWS MEO Violation Outcomes	218,841	65,810	30.1%

NOTE: Table excludes 7,307 Coast Guard active-duty members.

[8] Respondents were asked to report events that occurred between the date they took the survey and the same date one year earlier. We refer to this time period as the *past year*.

[9] Confidence intervals (CIs) describe how precisely one can draw inferences about the population from a statistic estimated on a sample from that population. For example, in the analytic sample of respondents 1.54 percent of active-duty service members indicated experiencing a sexual assault. We can infer from these respondents that the true percentage in the population falls between 1.38 percent and 1.70 percent with very high confidence (probability = .95). Larger samples allow for narrower confidence intervals.

[10] An implication of this strategy is that once a service member indicated having experienced a sexual assault during the past year, we did not continue to ask detailed questions that would have identified additional sexual assaults. A detailed analysis of the sexual assault instrument, including its correspondence with the specific wording of Article 120, is included in the RAND methodology report that will be released later.

[11] *Private areas* were defined to include the buttocks, inner thigh, breast, groin, anus, vagina, penis and testicles.

[12] In the field of epidemiology, the association between a risk factor and an outcome is often described in terms of a relative risk ratio, or the ratio of the probability of an event occurring in an exposed group relative to that in a group not exposed. Relative risk ratios of 5 or 10 are considered large (e.g., McMahon & Pugh, 1970). Our results suggest that the relative risk ratio of quid pro quo as a function of hostile work environment is 101.

[13] Precise estimates on sexual assault and sexual harassment from the 2012, 2010, and 2006 surveys were provided by DMDC to RAND for purposes of making these comparisons. Effects are referred to as significant with p<.05.

[14] In this section, we limit discussion of changes in rates over time to just those differences that are statistically significant, unless otherwise noted. Where we do not mention changes from a prior year administration of the WGRA, no significant differences were found between 2014 and that year.

[15] Such a question had not previously been included in the WGRA survey, and it represented the only item added to that survey in the 2014 RMWS.

[16] Although 19.8 percent of those counted as experiencing a past-year unwanted sexual contact cannot be counted as experiencing a penetrative, non-penetrative, or attempted sexual contact as their "one event," 14.6 percent of this number indicated "did not do this" for every type of sexual contact listed for establishing the USC type categorization. The remaining 5.2 percent skipped one or more items, and did not mark "yes" on any item they did not skip.

Abbreviations

CI	confidence interval
DoD	Department of Defense
DMDC	Defense Manpower Data Center
MEO	military equal opportunity
OSD	Office of the Secretary of Defense
OUSD/P&R	Office of the Under Secretary of Defense for Personnel and Readiness
RMWS	RAND Military Workplace Study
RR1	Response Rate 1 (as defined by the American Association of Public Opinion Research)
SAPRO	Sexual Assault Prevention and Response Office
UCMJ	Uniform Code of Military Justice
USC	United States Code
WGRA	Workplace and Gender Relations Survey of Active Duty Personnel